Welcome to
Mexico

by Alison Auch

Content and Reading Adviser: Mary Beth Fletcher, Ed.D.
Educational Consultant/Reading Specialist
The Carroll School, Lincoln, Massachusetts

D1528546

Spyglass
BOOKS

COMPASS POINT BOOKS

Minneapolis, Minnesota

Compass Point Books
3722 West 50th Street, #115
Minneapolis, MN 55410

Visit Compass Point Books on the Internet at *www.compasspointbooks.com*
or e-mail your request to *custserv@compasspointbooks.com*

Photographs ©: Dallas and John Heaton/Corbis, cover; Corel, cover (background), 6, 8, 9,
10, 12, 13, 15, 16, 17; Kelly-Mooney Photography/Corbis, 4; Macduff Everton/Corbis, 7;
Two Coyotes Studio/Mary Foley, 11; Tony Arruza/Corbis, 14.

Project Manager: Rebecca Weber McEwen
Editor: Heidi Schoof
Photo Selectors: Rebecca Weber McEwen and Heidi Schoof
Designers: Jaime Martens and Les Tranby
Illustrator: Svetlana Zhurkina

Library of Congress Cataloging-in-Publication Data

Auch, Alison.
  Welcome to Mexico / by Alison Auch.
     p. cm. — (Spyglass books)
Includes bibliographical references and index.
Contents: Where is Mexico? — City living — Wear it out! — Flat bread
— Party time! — "Rabbit and Coyote."
  ISBN 0-7565-0373-6 (hardcover)
  1. Mexico—Juvenile literature. 2. Mexico—Social life and
customs—Juvenile literature. [1. Mexico—Social life and customs.]
  I. Title. II. Series.
  F1208.5 .A93 2002
  972—dc21
                                        2002002753

Contents

Where Is Mexico? 4

At Home 6

At Work 8

Flat Bread 10

Clothing 12

Party Time! 14

Fun Facts 16

Rabbit and Coyote 18

Glossary 22

Learn More 23

Index 24

Where Is Mexico?

Welcome to my country!
I live in Mexico.
I want to tell you about
my beautiful home.

Mexican Flag

Did You Know?

Mexico has deserts, rain forests,
tall mountains, good farmland,
and white sandy beaches.

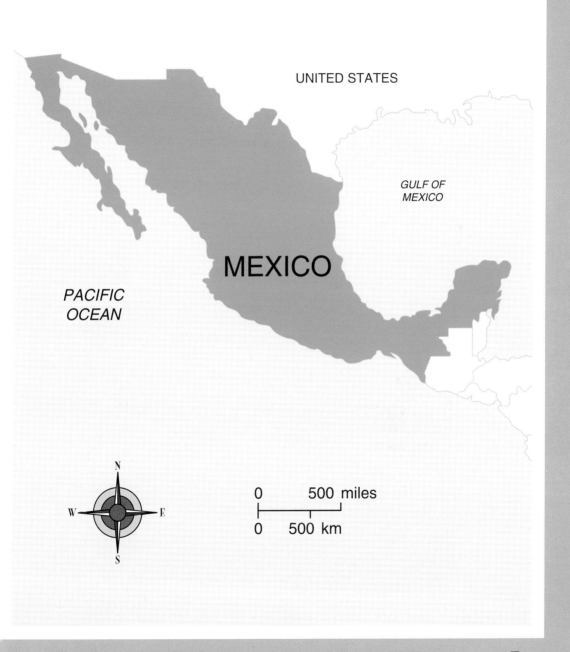

UNITED STATES

GULF OF
MEXICO

MEXICO

PACIFIC
OCEAN

N
W   E
S

0   500 miles
0   500 km

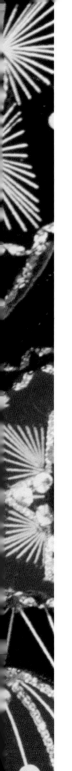

At Home

My family lives in Mexico City. We have a big apartment. My grandmother shares it with us.

Many people paint their homes bright colors in Mexico.

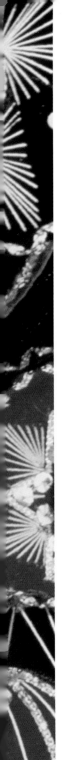

At Work

My family works hard.
My father has a restaurant.
My mother works in
a museum. My grandmother
takes care of us.

Grandmother and I can
buy almost anything at
the outdoor markets.

Flat Bread

In Mexico, we eat a lot of corn. We even use corn to make *tortillas.* We wrap the tortillas around beans or meat.

We like to put spicy chilies and garlic in our food.

Clothing

The weather here is warm so we wear clothes that keep us cool. I have to wear special clothes to school. When I get home, I change into jeans.

During special holidays, such as **Mexican Independence Day,** dancers wear traditional clothes.

Party Time!

When it is my birthday, we have a *piñata* filled with toys and candy. We take turns hitting the piñata until it breaks.

A piñata

On holidays and weekends,
we like to ride on boats like
this one in an old *Aztec canal.*

Fun Facts

Mexico City is the biggest city in the world. It also has the biggest traffic jams!

In some parts of Mexico, people have *iguanas* as pets.

In Mexico, many children wear uniforms to school

Mexico City is built on land that was once a lake. This is also where the Aztecs had their main city.

Some people use the leaves of prickly pear *cactus* in salads.

Rabbit and Coyote

Rabbit liked to trick Coyote. One night, he saw the moon was shining on a pond.

Rabbit told Coyote that the moon in the pond was cheese. He said Coyote could get the cheese if he drank all the water.

Coyote started drinking the water. He drank and drank. Soon he felt sick.

The water in the pond was almost gone. Coyote still could not get the cheese. Rabbit had tricked him again!

Glossary

Aztec–one of the native people who had a great civilization in central Mexico several hundred years ago

cactus–a desert plant with sharp needles growing out of it

canal–something that has been made so water can flow through it and carry boats

iguana–a big lizard

Mexican Independence Day–September 16, the day Mexicans celebrate their freedom from the country of Spain

piñata–a hollow shape filled with candy and treats

tortilla–flat bread made from corn or flour

Learn More

Books

Burr, Claudia, Krystyna Libura, and Cristina Urrutia. *Broken Shields.* Toronto, Ontario: Groundwood Books/Douglas & McIntyre, 1997.

Dahl, Michael. *Mexico.* Mankato, Minn.: Bridgestone Books, 1997.

Heinrichs, Ann. *Mexico.* New York: Children's Press, 1997.

Web Sites

www.ipl.org/youth/cquest

www.elbalero.gob.mx/index_kids.html

Index

Aztec, 15, 17

Gulf of Mexico, 5

iguana, 16

Mexican Independence Day, 13

Mexico City, 6, 16, 17

museum, 8

Pacific Ocean, 5

piñata, 14

prickly pear cactus, 17

GR: F
Word Count: 203

From Alison Auch

Reading and writing are my favorite things to do. When I'm not reading or writing, I like to go to the mountains or play with my little girl, Chloe.